Jens D. C. Lieblein

**Egyptian Religion**

Jens D. C. Lieblein

**Egyptian Religion**

ISBN/EAN: 9783337235604

Printed in Europe, USA, Canada, Australia, Japan

Cover: Foto ©Lupo / pixelio.de

More available books at **www.hansebooks.com**

# EGYPTIAN RELIGION

BY

## J. LIEBLEIN

PROFESSOR AT THE UNIVERSITY OF CHRISTIANIA.

———————

LEIPZIG.

I. C. HINRICHS'SCHE BUCHHANDLUNG.

1884.

science on religions is not possible. The sacred books of India have already been brought before the public. At the said Congress it was decided that all extant copies of the Egyptian sacred book called „The Book of Death" should be collected, so that a correct and entire edition of it might be available. This work is now nearly finished.

The sacred books of some nations were published long ago, and others will be so shortly. There is therefore every likelihood that Max Müllers idea will be realised within a time not far distant. And the man of science does not stand alone here in his eager researches: the educated public seems in a high degree to be interested in the work, and receives gladly the fruits of it. An instance of this is the work above mentioned. It will also, no doubt, be received with that approbation which it rightly deserves.

The most essential point in such works is that the facts be correctly stated. That such is the case with the present work is warranted by the circumstance, that the author is specially learned in the science in question. But just because that guarantee gives the reader confidence, so that he believes what he reads to be absolutely correct, I hope I shall be excused when, in my capacity of critic, I point out those places, which according to my opinion, may lead to erroneous views, and such places are to be found in the said work. The details, the facts, are generally correctly stated, but the conception and the leading thoughts are I should say occasionally wrongly expressed, a circumstance indifferent to the learned reader, but the more dangerous to the unscientific. We will point out some opinions to be found page 81.

The author says first: „The earliest monuments which have been discovered present to us the very same fully developed civilization and the same religion as the later monuments:" and further on he tries to illustrate this idea by adding: „The gods whose names appear in the oldest tombs were worshipped down to the Christian times. The same kind of priesthoods which are mentioned in the tablets of Canopus and Rosetta in the Ptolemaic period are as ancient as the Pyramids, and more ancient than any Pyramid of which we know the date."

From these words the general reader will doubtless receive the decided impression, that not only the profane civilization of the Egyptians but also their ideas on religious matters had remained unchanged i. e. that the Egyptian intellectual life was without progress, without advancement, without life during a period of four thousand years, during the whole historical existence of the Egyptian empire.

In my opinion it would be surprising, if a civilization that has advanced so far as the Egyptian, could have remained unchanged during four thousand years without progressing or retrograding. But, as regards more especially culture in general, viz. art and science, this is not the place for further explanation. I shall only remark in passing that, for instance in architecture, development

1*

is manifest from the raw square pillars in the tombs of
the third and fourth dynasties, to the colossal, and yet
so elegant columns in the Seti hall at Karnak: in astro-
nomy, the star observations in Bab-el-Moluk's tombs: in
medecine, the collection of medical writings in Papyrus
Ebers and the medical Papyrus in Berlin: in mathema-
tics, the mathematical Papyrus in London, clearly shows
a development from earlier, wavering stray attempts. It
is otherwise impossible. A cultured nation, as the Egyptians undoubtedly were, cannot remain stagnant during
the space of several thousand years. A general presumption is in any case insufficient: proof is required. Even
were we, for instance, able to point out one or more
works of sculpture from the earliest time, which have
not been surpassed later, this is no proof of stagnation
or decline, any more than the works of Homer or Phidias,
which still remain for us unrivalled, prove that our culture, taken as a whole, is below that of the Greeks.

But let us return to religion. That is for us the
essential point. The author says that „the earliest monuments present to us the same religion as the later monuments." And that „the gods whose names appear in the
oldest tombs, were worshipped down to the Christian
times."

The last sentence is true, if we take the words lite-
rally, but it is untrue, in so far, as it indirectly conceals,
that in later times there were added names of more gods,
and in so far as it is intended to prove the first state-

ment about the religion being unchanged. If it were true in other respects, it could at any rate not prove that the religion had continued the same from the oldest to the latest times. The Christian as well as the Jew certainly acknowledges that Jehovah gave Moses the tables of stone with the commandments written thereon, but Judaism and Christianity are not on that account the same religion, nor do the Jews and Christians, in the name Jehovah, have the same conception of God, he being for us, no longer, the exclusive God of the Jews. The Protestants as well as the Catholics acknowledge the Virgin Mary to be the mother of Christ, but for all that, Protestantism and Catholicism are not identical, neither does the Virgin Mary occupy the same position in the protestant church as in the catholic. The Christian, as well as the Jew and the Mohammedan, acknowledges Moses to be a man of God who delivered his people from the Egyptian thraldom, and they relate the same about the patriarchs Abraham, Isaac and Jacob, but Christianity, Judaism and Mohammedanism are not on that account the same religion, neither has the religious development remained stagnant from the time of these patriarchs through Judaism, Islam and Christianity up to the present time. The Mosaic law, the ten commandments, are certainly acknowledged as the highest moral guidance for Christians as well as for Jews, but notwithstanding this, the religion of the old and new Testaments are not one and the same, neither have the Jews the same ideas of the com-

mandments as the Christians, for whom „Love is the ful-
filling of the Law" and for whom „The Law was our
schoolmaster to bring us unto Christ." We see therefore that the same names do not always convey the same
ideas, and that the same thing is often not the same
thing. Likewise is it the case, or may be the case, with
the same names of gods, on the most ancient and the
newest Egyptian monuments. It is not necessary, that
they should signify the same conception of God, and it
is most probable that they do not; at any rate they can in
no way prove, that the Egyptian religion has remained
unchanged, during three to four thousand years.

Tiele says quite correctly, that in Egypt the old was
never put out by the new, but kept its place by its side:
if we add to this that the ideas on the old necessarily
were influenced by the new, then we have the key to the
correct views on the assumption of Le Page Renouf.
He says that the old gods were worshipped until the
latest times, but he forgets to add, that new gods were
in the meantime added, so that not only were the ideas
about the old gods modified, but the conception of the
deity had, on the whole, become more comprehensive and
enlarged: yes, he has forgotten it to such a degree that
he even straightforwardly denies the development, and
declares that the religion remained unchanged. The
author however seems himself to imply, that the religious life of the Egyptians, like all other life, has been
in progress and development, as he in another place

refers to the well known religious reformation which occurred under Amenofis the IV. and again in yet another place he speaks of a pantheistic period, and of how the Egyptians approached monotheism but fell into pantheism; but as he, in the words above quoted, in a decisive way declares the Egyptian religion to be unchanged, so it is necessary in an equally decisive manner to protest against these words, that they may not be interpreted to have more importance than the author has intended to give them, but which they on his authority might easily get.

I will not however restrict myself to a bare protest, but will try to find out the development that is the chief point to a man of research. Egyptian writings must of course be our source, and it must be our chief duty to adhere strictly to the time and the chronology, as the historical train of the development cannot otherwise be brought to light.

In the oldest tombs, where the oldest writings are found, there are not many gods mentioned — there are Osiris, Horus, Thot, Seb, Nut, Hathor, Anubis, Apheru and a couple more. Osiris, whose name probably signifies the seat of the eye, that is the sun eye, or the sun, was originally a god of the sun, the sungod in Abydos. Horus, his son, was the god in the height i. e. the sun, the sun of the day, that with farther reflection, was placed in contrast to Osiris, who thus became the sun of the night, the sun of the lower regions. Thot, or Tehuti, as the name is now usually read, was the god of the moon, Seb was the earth, Nut was the heaven, Hathor is the dwelling of Horus i. e. the firmament, Anubis was possibly, as Le Page Renouf believes, originally the twilight, but he has already in the tombs here mentioned got a fixed function in the lower regions, he being called, „The Lord of the grave," and he is the guide of the dead. Apheru is another form of Anubis, he opens the paths for the dead. These and some other gods such as Isis, the dawn of day, and Neith were thus chiefly gods of nature: some of them are however already losing this character in that they begin to take over other functions principally as funereal gods. Thus we see that these tombs are not devoid of the idea of a life hereafter, but a complete, fully developed doctrine had as yet certainly not gained general approbation, since it is a peculiarity of these graves in contrast to those of a later period. that writings of funereal or religious contents, as a rule, are so little conspicuous in them. Representations of the deceased's life in this world, as well as sacrifices to his honour and memory, form the chief interest, to which may be added, that the worship of deceased kings is often mentioned.

It will be seen from the above that the main objects of the religion, as represented in the oldest tombs, are the gods of nature, the worship of ancestors, and a dawning doctrine of a future life. This is the oldest feature of religion to be learned from the Egyptian monuments:

what lies before this is merely a subject for speculation, for more or less plausible guesswork.

Among the gods of nature, the sun plays a prominent part, and this is quite natural: the sun brings light, warmth, life and fertility. Osiris and Horus were, as we have seen, gods of the sun. Ra, whose name signifies sun, was the god of the sun in Heliopolis, and retained this character as god of the sun during the entire Egyptian history. From the most ancient times, already under the second dynasty, the kings took the name of Ra, and the Pharaos justified their godlike authority by calling themselves „Son of Ra". The other gods were identified with Ra being called Amon-ra, Sebek-ra, Num-ra, Hor-ra etc. This however first took place at a later period, than that, about which we are now speaking. The whole of the fifteenth chapter of the Book of Death is one single hymn to the sun: „the Lord of the heaven, the chief of the gods, who has created himself, and whom all gods rejoice in beholding."

But although the god of the sun was in a high degree prominent in ancient Egypt, and perhaps the most commonly worshipped, he was not the only god of nature. We have above also mentioned the earth — Seb — the heaven — Nut — and the moon — Thot. Thus on the lid of Menkera's coffin from the fourth dynasty we read as follows: „Oh! Menkera, thy mother, the firmament (Nut) spreads herself over thee in her name, the secret of the heaven. She has given it to thee to be as a god and that thy enemies shall be destroyed."

In consideration of this, I must firmly contest the idea, that the Egyptians commenced with monotheism, an opinion brought forward by De Rougé, or the idea that the most ancient religion of the Egyptians was the purest and most perfect, an opinion which Le Page Renouf propounds in his book page 91 where he says:

"It is incontestably true that the sublimer portions of the Egyptian religion are not the comparatively late result of a process of development or elimination from the grosser. The sublimer portions are demonstrably ancient."

On the contrary I nearly agree with the Dutch savant Tiele, when he describes the development of the Egyptian religion in the following true words:

"It is altogether wrong to consider the Egyptian religion as a polytheistic deviation from a pre-historic monotheism. It was from the beginning polytheistic, but developed into two opposite directions. On the one side, the world of the gods became more and more enriched by additions from the local religions, and by adopting strange gods, on the other side they approached monotheism, as it were gropingly, without ever declaring it unmistakeably and distinctly."

That doctrine is certainly abandoned long ago as antiquated, that the true religion, by a pre-historic revelation from the beginning, was dispersed among all people on earth. Assuredly there are not many now, who feel attracted by what, for instance Jablonski said 130 years ago, probably referring to this doctrine on the subject of the oldest Egyptian religion:

„As the first inhabitants of Egypt were descendants of Noah, his son Ham, and grandson Misraim, their religion after the deluge must have been true and pure, in that it was the revelation of God . . . . Every thing leads us therefore to believe, and proves in the most manifest way, that the knowledge of the only true God, and the worship of God, in keeping with that knowledge, prevailed in Egypt more than three hundred years after the deluge."

The science of religion does not any longer avow this doctrine, although it seems, in an unconscious and latent manner to bewilder people, where it should be least expected. No, the Egyptians have without doubt, as all other heathen nations, by their own help, been obliged to work out their views on divinity. In this respect, we can fortunately also appeal to Max Müller's weighty authority.

It is however not my opinion that it is possible in any people hitherto historically known, to show the first origin of the idea of God. When we, for instance, take the Indo-europeans, what do we find there? the Sanscrit word deva is identical with the Latin deus, and the northern tivi, tivar; as now the word in Latin and northern language signifies God it must also in Sanscrit from the beginning have had the same signification. That

is to say the Arians, or Indo-europeans, must have com-
bined the idea of God with this word, as early as when
they still lived together in their original home. Because,
if the word in their pre-historic home had had another
more primitive signification, the wonder would have
happened, that the word had accidentally gone through
the same development of signification with all these
people after their separation. As this is quite improbable,
the word must have had the signification of God in
original Indo-european language. One could go even farther and presume that, in this language also, it was a
word derived from others, and consequently originated
from a still earlier pre-historic language. All things considered it is possible, even probable, that the idea of
God has developed itself in an earlier period of languages,
than the Indo-european. The future will perhaps be able
to supply evidence for this.

The science of languages has been able partly to reconstruct an Indo-european pre-historic language. It might
perhaps be able also to reconstruct a pre-historic Semitic,
and a pre-historic Hamitic, and of these three pre-historic
languages, whose original connexion it not only guesses,
but even commences to prove gradually, it will, we trust
in time, be able to extract a still earlier pre-historic
language, which according to analogy might be called
Noahitic. When we have come so far, we shall most
likely in this pre-historic language, also find words ex-
pressing the idea of God. But it is even possible that

the idea of God has not come into existence in this prehistoric language either. It may be that the first dawning of the idea, and the word God should be ascribed to still earlier languages, to layers of languages so deeply buried that it will be impossible ever to excavate them. Between the time of inhabiting caves in the quaternian period, and the historical kingdoms, there is such a long space of time, that it is difficult to entertain the idea, that it was quite devoid of any conception of divinity, so that this should first have sprung up in the historical time.

In any case we shall not be able to prove historically, where and when the question first arose, who are the superhuman powers whose activity we see daily in nature and in human life. Although the Egyptians are the earliest civilized people known in history, and just therefore especially important for the science of religion, yet it is even there impossible to point out the origin of the conception of the deity.

The oldest monuments of Egypt bring before us the gods of nature chiefly, and among these especially the sun. They mention however already early (in the fourth and fifth dynasties) now and then the great power, or the great God, it being uncertain whether this refers to the sun, or another god of nature, or if it was a general appellation of the vague idea of a supernatural power, possibly inherited by the Egyptians. It is probably this great God indicated on the monuments, from the fourth dynasty, and later on, who has given occasion to the false belief, that the oldest religion of the Egyptians was pure monotheism. But firstly it must be observed, that he is not mentioned alone but alongside of the other gods, secondly that he is merely called „The great God" being otherwise without distinguishing appellations, and a God of whom nothing else is mentioned, has, so to speak to use Hegels language, merely an abstract existence, that by closer examination dissolves into nothing.

This undefined „great God" could only, by being placed alongside of other distinct gods, get a distinct full character: it was merely through polytheism that true monotheism could come into existence.

On the monuments from the fourth and fifth dynasty the memphitic local god Ptah likewise begins to make his appearance. He was also, according to Le Page Renouf's opinion, originally a god of the sun but became, as the name indicates, very early the god that opens. that reveals himself in his creation. Furthermore, the god Set is to be found in the pyramid tombs. He represents, according to Le Page Renouf, darkness and became thus a contrast to the god of the sun. Partly on this account, partly also, perhaps, because he was originally identical with a Semitic god, he was at last considered a bad spirit. When I now lastly mention the bull Apis who is called „Ptahs other life" and was also an incarnation of Ptah, then we have mentioned nearly all the gods known to the four or five first dynasties.

I dare not however pretend that I have included all, as this is the first attempt at a chronological arrangement. The number of gods increased very rapidly, as the local gods of different districts and towns when Egypt became a united kingdom came forward, and insisted on being acknowledged. These local gods were all principally the same gods of nature, especially gods of the sun, which we have met before, only with different names. But as the priests at the union of Egypt little by little tried to collect them in a common official circle of gods, it became necessary to ascribe to them different qualities and functions, whereby their nature in course of time was changed, in that they became representatives for the different sides in the conception of deity now developing more and more fully. We can point out traces of this process in the pyramid tombs. The Memfitic sun god Ptah is he who opens, shapes and forms, that is the artist, the god with the beautiful look, the god of beauty. The Thinitic sun god Osiris, succeeded by his son Horus in his function as the sun of the day, has become the sun of the night, the sun in the lower regions, furthermore Lord of the lower regions, and finally he has, as representative for the ethic side of the deity, become the judge over the dead in the lower regions. The god of the moon, Tehuti is first he, who measures time, the Lord of days, weeks, months and seasons, then he, who has measured the heaven, and numbered the stars, measured the earth, and numbered the things that are thereon, finally, the inventor of letters, literature and science.

During the sixth dynasty we observe further progress. In the newly discovered pyramids belonging to king Pepi and his son Merenra are found the following expressions: „Horus, his father's avenger", and speaking to his father Osiris: „I have fought for thee, I have avenged thee father Osiris on those who have injured thee." Here we have one of the earliest references to the Osiris myth, that describes the strife between the light, Osiris, and the darkness, Set. We see here the idea of God developing still further, as it comprises the contrast between light and darkness, good and evil, life and death.

Not until the 11th and 12th dynasties, in the second thousand years after the foundation of the empire by Menes, the Theban gods such as Mont, Ammon, and others, begin to appear on the monuments. Mont was originally a local sun god but changed at an early period into a god of strength, a god of strife and war. If Ammon was from the beginning a god of nature, we do not know; if he had ever been that, he had at all events lost this character by the time the monuments introduce him to us. He was, according to the signification of the word, the secret and the mysterious, therefore not at all a god of nature, who could be touched or felt by the help of the senses. He betokens consequently a very important advancement in the conception of the deity, showing that the Egyptians at the time of the 11th dynasty had risen to the acknowledgment of a superhuman God, who was hidden, as it were, concealed behind nature, the world we see and feel. It was likewise to Ammon, that the Egyptians later on under their progressing development naturally attached their purest monotheistic conception of deity, as may be seen from the hymns of the 18th and later dynasties, of which I shall further on give an exemple. If we look back upon the development from the first dynasties on to the 11th and 12th dynasties or the first fifteen hundred years, what do we then find? When we keep strictly to the chronological tables, and do not in a bewildering manner mix times and places, as is so often infortunately the case in illustrating the Egyptian religion, then the monuments will convince us, that the conception of deity became more elevated and distinct at the same time, that the original gods of nature changed from objects perceived by the senses into spiritual beings. This development has certainly its deepest reason in the manner in which the idea of God logically worked itself out, but was helped forward no doubt by the circumstance, that different local gods by the union of the districts into one kingdom were collected together into one official circle or complex of gods, whereby several chiefly identical gods of nature had to be attributed different qualities and functions.

But here we have to observe another important fact. In the official religion of the state the different local gods were melted together into one complex of gods

with the local god of the metropolis at the head of them;
but in the different districts the worship continued of
the respective local gods, each of which was by his
worshippers considered to be the only and highest God,
the other local gods not being taken into consideration.
While in this way the religion of the state (if I may
express myself in this manner) spiritualised the conception
of the deity, that is transformed the poor gods of nature into
spiritual beings of a richly developed type, the monotheism
progressed by the worship in the districts. Here again
we see a casual circumstance that greatly contributed to
heighten and make perfect the ideas of the deity with
the priests and the educated classes.

In this the development progressed quickly and surely,
so that certain schools and classes of the people, under
the 18th and 19th dynasties could acknowledge pure
monotheism. It is thus from this period the doctrine
of one God originates, and it is to the religion of this
period that the characteristic applies, that Le Page Renouf
quotes after De Rougé page 89: „God. One, Sole and
Only; no others with Him. — He is the Only Being —
living in truth. — Thou art One, and millions of beings
proceed from thee. — He has made everything, and he
alone has not been made. The clearest, the simplest,
the most precise conception."

In a hymn to Ammon not older than the 18th dynasty,
it is said about Ammon, that he has created men, beasts
and things that exist, that he has made the trees to

grow, the grass to sprout and the animals to live, that
he has produced everything that is above, and that is
beneath, that he gives light to the earth, and flies through
the heaven in peace, that he is one and alone, and that
his equal is not to be found.

The historical progress of development here shown, is
supported, as far as I can see, by the monuments, and I
will therefore suggest to the honourable author if he
should not after renewed deliberation find reason to modify
his assertion on the Egyptian religion's unchangeableness,
and his words „That the sublimer portions of the Egyptian
religion are not a result of a process of development or
elimination from the grosser."

I will of course not deny that a single, gifted, clear
seeing genius, even before that time, might have acknowledged God as one, but I firmly assert, that a monotheistic doctrine generally introduced and believed in by
numbers did not appear before the 18th dynasty, or about
that period.

This and this alone can explain how Amenofis the
fourth, one of the 18th dynasty's last kings could try
his religious reformation and carry it successfully through.
When he began his reign, the religion of the people
continued of course to be polytheistic, it being only in
the learned schools and among the higher classes, that
monotheism had found entrance. But king Amenofis, who
was an eager adherent of the new religion, introduced
monotheism as the religion of the state. He put aside

2*

all these many gods, he prosecuted especially the Theban Ammon, who being the local god of the metropolis was at that time at the head of the official complex of gods, and consequently enjoyed the highest esteem. Instead of this he introduced the worship of one only God whom he named Khu-en-aten, or as I believe the name should rather be read, Aten-khu-n-ra, i. e. the disk of the sun, the god of the sun's brightness. It was thus the belief in the original sungod he reintroduced, with however a difference chiefly in the understanding of it. It was not any longer the material sun, whose light and warmth are felt by the senses, but a spiritual being, a concealed God, who only reveals himself through the disk of the sun, and who lends his brightness to the sun.

The new religion did not last long, as the old polytheism with its pompous ceremonies had taken too deep root with the people. Only the reformer himself and a couple of his nearest successors were able to uphold the monotheistic religion, after which time the old polytheism was again installed. But even although the attempt had at last to be given up, it stands as a manifestation and proof of how the religious life was in commotion, and how generally adopted monotheism must in those days have been by the higher classes in Egypt.

This is however not the only manifestation of monotheism. In another place I have tried to show that the priests in Heliopolis, at about the same time, or more

correctly, a little earlier had raised themselves to adopt
the doctrine of a monotheistic God, which they called
Khepera, i. e. the God who is, who exists, a name
that has the same derivation and meaning in the Egyptian
language as Jahwe has in the Hebrew. I will not here
repeat my arguments, but only state that in the god
Khepera we have, at least in my opinion, a new manifestation of the monotheistic doctrine, at that period so
widely spread.

When monotheism was reached, the highest step in
the conception of the deity was arrived at. The original
gods of nature had during the progressing development
more and more become spiritual powers, that were mysteri-
ously placed behind the world we see and feel, until they
were at last moulded together into one only God, that
stood beyond the world, and in contrast to it. But no
sooner had the development reached monotheism, when
the opposite process set in. Through pantheism God
was again drawn into the world in that he was believed
to penetrate everything, both man and beast, so that
nothing was without God as is said in the 42nd chapter
of the Book of Death. Hereby the road was opened for
the most bewildering polytheism, and for the coarsest
superstition that is characteristic of the last stage of the
Egyptian religion, as we learn from Greek and Roman
authors, though it might be possible that pantheism, or
perhaps more correctly expressed, the doctrine of emanation may on the other hand have paved the way for instance

for the Christian doctrine, that God has become man. I shall not further dwell on this retrograde movement. It is in this place my chief object to show the course of the progressing development to supplement Le Page Renouf's writings on the subject in which the development is not only neglected, but even positively denied.

Without tarrying farther with my inability to understand in what light they look upon history in general, or the Egyptian history of religion in particular, when they assume such a denial, I shall, to demonstrate and prove my opinion on the subject, also take the Book of Death as my guide for deliberation — this book being the actual sacred book of the Egyptians.

The writings of the Book of Death from different times show that it consists of a primitive text and of the writings of the 1st, 2nd and 3th commentators; these four different parts represent consequently just as many steps in the development of the religious ideas. The much honoured veteran of the Egyptologists, Lepsius, published long ago the oldest writings of the Book of Death. These are from the time of the 11th and 12th dynasties, but the original text is not given here pure as traces are found of additions from the 1st and 2nd commentators, meanwhile we can infer pretty nearly the words of the original writings. As the Theban local god Ammon is not mentioned in the Book of Death until in the latest additions, the primitive writings must have been compiled in the Memphitic period, thus probably before the end of the 6th dynasty. Even if it does not represent the earliest religious state of the Egyptians, which, as we have already shown, we must look for in the oldest pyramid tombs, it is still of a very good age. It is, more correctly defined, an expression of the henotheistic period, which began when the different local gods came up together, each demanding exclusively to be acknowledged as the principal and the highest god. This is clearly shown by the 17th chapter, one of the oldest parts of the Book of Death. The deceased here identifies himself with God i. e. for prudence sake with everyone of the henotheistic gods, in that he says:

„I am Tum; I am Ra in his first appearance; I am the great God who has created himself; I am the great Bennu who is in On; I am Khem in his appearance."

The gods here mentioned were local gods of nature, that by accident were placed together and of which each was worshipped as the principal and only God. This is however not monotheism but henotheism, as Max Müller calls it.

Let us now consider the commentators. They stand on a higher eminence of culture.

The primitive words are: „I am Tum". An interpreter adds to this: „I was one I", and another: „In heaven's ocean". The whole sentence sounds thus in a later edition: „I am Tum, who was alone in the heaven's ocean" and reminds us of Genesis I, 2nd: „And the spirit of God moved upon the face of the waters."

After this it is said in the original writings: „I am Ra in his first appearance". To this a commentator adds: „He gilds the horizon in the 'morning". Other commentators make different additions such as: „In the beginning of his reign", and „I lifted up the heaven's ocean". This reminds us of the 1st and 2nd days of the creation in Genesis: „And there was light". „And God made the firmament, and divided the waters which were under the firmament from the waters that were above the firmament" . . . . . . „And God called the firmament heaven". To „lift up the heaven's ocean" is, we may understand, to make a firmament below the waters above.

Further, the original text says as follows: „I am the great God who has created himself." To this a commentator adds: „It is the water, the heaven's ocean, the father of the gods", and another commentator: „It is Ra".

Further, the original text says as follows: „I am the great Bennu, who is in On". To this the oldest commentator adds: „Examining that which is." Another says: „It is Osiris in On, it is his body, for ever and ever." And yet a third says: „That which is eternal is the day and that which is everlasting is the night".

Finally the original text says as follows: „I am Khem in his appearance, there are given unto me two feathers on my head." One commentator adds: „Khem is Horus, his father's avenger. The two feathers are the two uræus-serpents on his father Tum's forehead", and another: „The two feathers are Isis and Nefthys who

stand behind him in the capacity of twin sisters." A third
one: „His two eyes are the two feathers on his head."
This must be sufficient to show that every later
commentator adds something new. We have here passed
henotheism, and are on the stadium of the religion of
the state, where the different gods arranged in one complex are attributed different functions and qualities, or
are identified with each other. It may also be remarked here
that the later commentators are often more difficult to
understand than their predecessors, which no doubt can
be ascribed to the fact that the conception of the deity in
the course of time has been enriched through myths and
inspired by philosophy.

From the preceding we can clearly see that the Book
of Death proves, that there has been a progressing development in the religious life of the Egyptians. Further
demonstration in this respect will I hope be superfluous,
at the same time, it would be out of place now that we
may expect that the Geneva Egyptologist Naville will
shortly give us a far more complete compendium of the
Book of Death, than that we now possess.

In yet another respect a development can be shown.
This is in the Egyptian doctrine of another life, of
immortality, which also arose little by little.

I have already observed, that in the oldest tombs
we find very little in the way of funereal and religious
writings, a circumstance the more strange since the
later tombs are filled with them. Even although the

former are likewise filled with drawings and inscriptions, but the chief subjects of these are sacrifices to the deceased, and representations of his life on earth. We here see him (to refer to the last mentioned representations) in his full business on earth. He stands for instance watching his secretaries note down the number of his cows, asses, sheep and goats. He stands contemplating how the districts and places under his supervision, personified as women, bring forward their offerings or tithes: we see him shooting, fishing, sailing and rowing on the Nile: we see his people occupied ploughing and digging the soil, shearing corn, binding it in sheaves, carrying it home and threshing it, attending to the various domestic animals, milking the cows, loading and driving the asses, gathering the fruit from trees and bushes, pressing the juice from the fruit, catching fish and birds in nets, and slaughtering cattle. We see how the Egyptian who died five thousand years ago amuses himself with what his modern successor calls to this day „fantasia", he being present at his servant's or subject's playing of the harp and flute, their singing, their dancing, their games on the board and all kinds of gymnastic feats.

The other kind of representations illustrating the sacrifices are quite as conspicuous and numerous, and are to us at present of greater importance because they are if not precisely funereal, still of a certain funereal character. Before the deceased is placed the offering table, upon which are heaped a quantity of offerings, such as legs and heads of oxen, geese, different kinds of bread, vases and crocks with wine, incense etc. The inscriptions adjoining, that are arranged either in columns or in tablets give the name and the number of the offerings: incense, fruits, such as pomegranates, apricots, figs, grapes, wine, oil, different kinds of birds, each with its name and image, many kinds of bread and cakes, as well as innumerable other things. These offerings were to be brought at set times during the year as we see from the usual inscriptions: „May the offerings be given to the dead at the beginning of the year of the sun, on the first day of the civil year, at the feast of Thot, at the feast of Uaka, at the appearance of Sekhem, at the feast of Uab-akh, every month and every half month."

The worship of the dead was thus generally prevalent. It follows however from the nature of the case that offering to the dead was usually a private affair that only concerned the family. The festivals of sacrifice in honour of the deceased Pharaohs, must on the contrary have been an affair of the state. We find also very frequently priests mentioned, who in keeping with their title had priestly functions, at the pyramids of the kings. — Such priestly titles occur so frequently that we have every reason to presume that to every pyramid i. e. to every royal burying-place were attached one or more priests whose chief duty most likely was to preside over the sacrifices to the dead.

These funereal offerings, this worship of the dead,

of the ancestors, do not require to be connected with any doctrine regarding a future life, as these sacrifices may have been held to the honour and pious memory of the beloved deceased. But the pyramids, these immense royal burying-places, the erection of which cost such an amount of labour, had they not a religious signification? Should they not for instance preserve the body for a resurrection to a new life? Possible this was the intention especially in later times, but in the commencement pyramids were doubtless only monuments erected to the honour and memory of the deceased Pharaoh, or as the inscriptions say that his name might live in the future to everlasting time, and finally in order to have a place, where his sacrificial feasts might be kept. It can certainly not be denied, that it was Pharaoh himself who erected his own pyramid, he began it when he ascended the throne, and continued the building of it during his whole reign; but this was naturally, that he might be certain it should be carried on, which he could not be, were he to leave it to his successor's choice or will.

It is however not my meaning to pretend, that the Egyptians from the time of the oldest tombs, had no idea whatsoever of a future life. They were acquainted, as before stated with Anubis and Apheru, both funereal gods who opened the way for the dead and served them as guides on their path from this life to the other; it must not be omitted either, that in the tombs we not unfrequently find the prayer added, that the deceased may walk in the glorious way of the blessed. But a complete, fully developed and thoroughly consequent doctrine of the future state they cannot have had, as the oldest tombs show us nothing of this, and yet it is just in the tombs, where in later times the doctrine of immortality with its rewards and punishments is most extensively represented, and where properly speaking no other topic is treated besides death and the life after death.

In the oldest graves we find thus the doctrine of immortality only vaguely hinted at, while the worship of the dead, which as we have seen is very prominent, chiefly aimed at the preservation of their memory here on earth, although I will not entirely deny that the sacrifices to the dead might also at the same time (in the beginning perhaps vaguely) be intended to reconcile and please the dead.

The profane inscriptions in the tombs continue right on to the time of the Hyksos; but in the 6th dynasty (about 2500 years before Christ) a change took place as at that period biographical communications began to come into use. A high official called Una, who lived under the first three or four kings of the sixth dynasty, relates for instance his life's history in a rather explicit manner. He tells of the splendid career he has had, and the great deeds he has performed. By his lord the king's command he brought limestone from Troia (close by the Cairo of the present day) granite from Syene and alabaster from Hanub (near Siut), all of which were to be used for Pharaoh's tomb. No one can be surprised that Una in those days of king worship looked upon these purely private services performed for Pharaoh as being so important that the memory of them should be preserved forever. He accomplished however more important deeds: he was placed at the head of an army of „several myriads‟ which he had to drill, feed and clothe before he could lead them against the enemies of the country. These, Arabs and Beduins, were conquered, their fields destroyed, their vineyards and plantations cut down, their dwellings burned, their leaders killed and a host of captives made. For his private and public merits he was richly recompensed by Pharaoh, and „he was more pleasing to Pharaoh's heart than any other official or servant in the country.‟ But his like had never been seen and „there have never been such deeds performed in this country.‟

In Benihassan's tombs from the 12th dynasty similar biographies are found of great importance to history, but as they do not exactly bear upon our present topic I shall not deal farther with them. They can only here be of interest in so far as they show that the profane element still plays an important part in the tombs 2200 years before Christ. But the religious and funereal elements press little by little forward beside the profane, until at last from the 19th dynasty it becomes the overruling element in the inscriptions on the tombs.

We have already seen, when we spoke of the development of the conception of the deity, that during the 6th dynasty great progress was made. The same was the case with the doctrine of immortality, and both are deduced from the same Pepi's and Merenra's pyramids. We read thus in Merenra's pyramid the following, it being the god Horus who addresses the late Pharaoh Merenra:

„I stand with thee my father! I stand with thee Osiris, Merenra! I am thy son, I am Horus, I am coming to thee. Thou art purified and clean, risen again to life. Thou hast gathered together thy bones, fetched back what had gone from thee, collected together what has issued from thee, I am Horus my father's avenger, I have fought for thee when thou wast beaten, I have avenged thee, father Osiris Merenra on those who have given thee pain, I have come to thee as attendant in the heaven, giving thee offering of incense, father Osiris Merenra; as thou sittest on the throne of the god Ra-Tum. Thou wanderest in the light of the sun, thou goest on board the ship of the sun beloved of the gods, in its cabin beloved of the gods, in that the god of the sun goes on board and sails with it. When the day breaketh Merenra goes on board. See he sitteth on the seat of the god of the sun, and proclaimeth his commands to the gods. See the god of the sun goes forth out of the lap of Nut, and is born every day, also Merenra is born every day as the sun. I have given to thee thy father Seb's inheritance among the gods in Heliopolis.“

We see here immortality distinctly proclaimed. The

dead becomes like unto God. He becomes Osiris and he is like Osiris, father to the god Horus; he is pure and holy, risen again to life, and in possession of his limbs; he is avenged by Horus who is his father's and consequently likewise his avenger; offerings of incense are brought him while he sits on the throne of the god of the sun; he goes in the boat of the sun and sails with the sun on the heaven's ocean.

Nearly the same doctrine is found, as before stated, in the beginning of the 17th chapter of the Book of Death. That was probably composed at the same time i. e. towards the end of the 6th dynasty.

Man should after death sail like a god in the boat of the sun, in blessed companionship with the god of the sun and his suite; this was the doctrine of immortality, which from this time was preached in the church of the state and was most generally and longest believed by the mass of the people. In the course of time different dogmas, different schools and different times appeared.

In connection with this general doctrine of immortality arose later on the doctrine of judgment in the other world, as it is represented in the 125th chapter of the Book of Death. To become blessed the deceased must have conducted himself in this life in a manner to deserve it. In the beginning this was either a matter of course, or had not been a subject of consideration. It was only after the notions on morality had been suffi-

ciently developed, and after one had come to a clear
understanding about right and wrong, bad and good, about
the justice of retribution, either as reward or punishment
in the other life, that the 125th chapter's doctrine of
judgement could come into existence, and this chapter
is plainly from a later period as Lepsius has shown; we
may even say that it was first composed in the time after
the expulsion of the Hyksos. Its contents are so generally known that no detailed account is here needed —
only some few words. Drawings and inscriptions corroborate each other, so the meaning is obvious. The drawing
represents a tribunal; Osiris presides as chief judge, on either side of him are seated 21 gods as judges, in front
there is a pair of scales in which the gods Horus and Anubis
are weighing the heart of the deceased in one scale against
the symbol of justice in the other, the god Thot writes
down the result. The goddess of justice lead the deceased forward to the tribunal and he commences his
speech according to the inscription in the following words:

„Be saluted, you lords of justice! be saluted thou
great lord of justice! I come to thee my lord! I am led
forward to behold thy glory! I know thee, I know thy.
name. I know the names of these thy 42 gods who are
with thee in the great hall of justice, who live to keep
guard over sinners, and to devour their blood on the day
when they shall make up their accounts to the god Un-
nofer."

He cleanses himself thereafter from sin naming each

of the 42 gods by name, and proclaims himself innocent of the special sin for which each god should punish. We have here the so-called negative register of sins, which shows us, that the moral law of the Egyptians contained 42 commandments whose chief contents are essentially identical with those in the Mosaic law.

Out of this doctrine of just retribution in the other world, that could naturally not only consists of reward but also of punishment, a new series of developments arose as a matter of course. To arrive at a clear understanding regarding the condition of the blessed in a future state had long been a subject of research; but what kind of punishments there were, and what the condition of the condemned would be, there was no call to consider, and about this we do not get direct information in the Book of Death, on the simple ground that by the book left by the relatives with the dead in the tomb it was piously presumed that he would be acquitted in the other world, and consequently become blessed. At last however the necessity was felt of becoming more acquainted with this subject. And we see thus that under the 18th dynasty vague foreshadowings of a doctrine of punishment began to appear, and from the 19th dynasty this topic was more and more explicitly treated. In the graves, in the sarcophaguses, in the papyrus literature, from this and later times we find ample information, as to what the Egyptians conceived punishment in the other world to be. The book on the infernal regions especially gives us full accounts.

It treats of the sun's nightly course; in the course of its wandering the sun comes to the dwellings of the condemned, which is now described. Drawing and inscriptions corroborate each other. One drawing shows us the condemned swimming in a lake of fire wherein their bodies burn without being consumed. Another represents several lakes of fire wherein the unhappy are tortured, while the fire is kept up by spirits who stand around, and spout out glowing venom into the lakes. The inscription teaches us the same. In one place it is said, addressing these spirits: „It is your function in the infernal regions to guard the places where the wicked are tortured in the fire according to the commands of the god Ra."

In another part the condemned are addressed as follows: „You are decapitated, you do not exist, your soul is annihilated; it cannot live on account of that which you have committed against my father Osiris." The torturings were as will be seen of different descriptions, but the fire is spoken of firstly and lastly and plays the principal part; and it is most likely this fire of the Egyptians that even now, as a phantom, survives in the modern cruel doctrine of hell fire. In any case, it is in Egypt that this doctrine can for the first time be historically proved.

We see thus wherever we turn: in the historical development of the conception of God, in the manner in which the Book of Death (the Egyptian Bible) came into existence, the teaching of morality and immortality, partly a movement forwards, partly after the highest point had been attained, a retrograding movement, from which however something new arose. This alone has made the Egyptians a nation of culture, whose life and history it is important to become acquainted with.

It is on this account that I have deemed it my duty to protest against Le Page Renouf's assertion that the Egyptian civilization and religion have remained unchanged through the course of time, an assertion that is dangerous, as it not only leads to misunderstanding Egyptian history, but also to the denial of the life principle in every history, to wit development and progress, without which life has no value.

I will now pass on to another part of Le Page Renouf's book where there are assertions, which I regard as incorrect, and which ought to be met with protest, as they might easily be considered as proved facts when taken on his authority. I refer to that part which commences page 243 where he deals with „Certain questions which have naturally arisen as to the influence of Egyptian upon foreign thought, as, for instance, on the Hebrew or Greek religions and philosophies." The author decides boldly this difficult and far-reaching question, that according to the opinion of other scientific investigators is by no means ripe for final settlement, in the following positive words: „It may be confidently asserted that neither Hebrews nor Greeks borrowed any of their ideas from Egypt." I can not approve of this answer.

Although I am still inclined to believe that the Biblical record of Moses having been educated in all the wisdom of Egypt is not a mere fable, and that this education proved useful to him during his later function as his people's deliverer and lawgiver, yet I shall not repeat what I have related elsewhere regarding the influence of the Egyptians on the Jews, but pass at once to the Greeks where that influence is more manifest.

I will not say positively that old Herodotus is on his part more correct when he states, that nearly all names of gods have come from Egypt to Hellas; for although he was 2000 years nearer the events than our highly esteemed English author he was evidently an Egyptoman, and Røth — sad to say — who tried to propound a similar opinion to Herodotus, made such a complete failure that he ought to be a warning example. But let us not on the other side go too far in our denial. It is easy to deny but we cannot come at the truth in that way. Here we must compare, investigate, and consider carefully and laboriously.

Le Page Renouf says that the Greeks have not borrowed religious ideas from Egypt. Not intending to be diffuse I shall restrict myself to the following remarks.

As to the earlier period, the mythological names Jo, Themis, and Kerberos have all an unmistakeable Egyptian stamp.

As to a later period I must draw attention to the worship of Zeus-Ammon which according to the latest investigations of Lepsius cannot have been any other than the Egyptian Ammon worship, introduced over Ammonium and Kyrene to Greece where the Egyptian Ammon had long ago been identified with the Greek Zeus.

As to the latest period I must point out the Greek-Roman Isis and Serapis worship; that it was introduced from Egypt is, as far as I am aware, at present acknowledged by all.

This must certainly be considered a loan and it is the Greeks who have borrowed from the Egyptians and not the other way. I must therefore firmly protest against the author's assertion that the Greeks have not borrowed religious ideas from the Egyptians, or it may be that his assertion is not so seriously meant? One might almost believe such to be the case; because in page 131 he compares the words e m h o t e p, that signifies „in peace" so often found in the Egyptian tombs, to similar inscriptions found in Hebrew and Christian tombs, and adds:

„It is extremely frequent in Egyptian texts, and may really be the origin of the Jewish and Christian form of petition for the departed, though the primitive signification has been altered."

Here the author himself speaks of loan, and as he can scarcely assert that such an odd fragment has been detached and alone brought over from Egypt to Europe, it seems to imply the acknowledgment that perhaps entire series of ideas are borrowed.

In addition to the above mentioned assertion the author says as follows page 246 sq.:

„Every step in the history of Greek philosophy can be accounted for and explained from native sources, and it is not merely unnecessary, but impossible (to the historian of philosophy, ridiculously impossible), to imagine a foreign teacher, to whom the Greeks would never have listened, as being the author of doctrines which without his help the Greeks would themselves certainly have discovered, and at the very time that they did so. The importance of Alexandria as a medium of interchange of ideas between the Eastern and Western worlds must also be considered as exploded. Nothing was more common, about forty or fifty years ago, than to hear learned men account for the presence of Oriental ideas in Europe, by the transmission of these ideas through the channel of Alexandria. Alexandria was supposed to be the seat of Oriental philosophy, and Philo, Origen, Porphyry, Plotinos and other great names, were imagined to be the representatives of the alliance between Greek and Oriental thought. All this is now considered as unhistorical as the reign of Jupiter in Crete. It was a mere a priori fancy, which has not been verified by facts. The most accurate analysis of the Alexandrian philosophy has not succeeded in discovering a single element in it which requires to be referred to an Oriental source. All attempts to refer Alexandrian opinions to Eastern sources have proved abortive. And long before the great work

of Zeller on Greek Philosophy had dealt with the problem
in detail, M. Ampère has shown how extremely improbable
the received hypothesis was. Alexandria was a commercial
Greek town, inhabited by a population which cared not
the least for Eastern ideas. The learned men in it were
Greeks who had the utmost contempt for barbarians and
their opinions. Of the Egyptian language and literature,
they were profoundly ignorant."

One is doubtless astonished on reading this. I have
quoted so much because I presume that I should not be
believed were I to use my own words in relating what
the author says. Does the author really mean that
the ideas in the Alexandrian philosophy are exclusively
Greek? When Philo makes allegories referring to the Old
Testament on the sacred writings of the Jews, which he
considers comprise all knowledge, and which he looks
upon as devoid of all error and imperfection, on account
of the divine revelation, does he not then supercede the
sources of Greek origin? Even Zeller, whom Le Page
Renouf quotes as one of his authorities, does not agree
with him, for in his great work on Greek philosophy he
has a long section entitled the Jewish-Greek philosophy,
to which among other men of learning the said Philo
belonged, and for whom, according to Zeller, the chief
basis was the Jewish religion, to the clearer understanding of which philosophy should be a mean of help. If
the author desires to have Zeller on his side, he must
admit that the Alexandrian philosophy sprang at least

from one foreign source viz. the Jewish, and he must not consider it „ridiculously impossible" that a foreign teacher, to whom the Greeks really listened, was the author of doctrines that the Greeks had certainly not discovered without his help. Philo was a Jew and the ideas of his philosophy was chiefly Jewish Oriental, but as regards language, the scientific form and method, he belonged to the Greek school, and was consequently acknowledged by the Greeks as one of themselves.

Is it reasonable to say that „the learned men of Alexandria were Greeks, who had the utmost contempt for barbarians and their opinions," when the ancient authors tell us (and we have no grounds to doubt their statements) that the Greek Ptolemies collected all they could lay hands on of foreign literature, had the Old Testament translated into Greek, and induced the Egyptian priest Manetho to write his country's history in Greek from Egyptian sources? And when the Jewish element played a part in the learned world of Alexandria, is it then probable that the Egyptian, which in the capital of Egypt, and for the scientifically interested Ptolemies was nearer at hand, should be of no importance? Zeller certainly believes this to be the case and his authority is weighty in these matters. He expresses himself however sometimes rather vaguely, his apprehension depends on his limited knowledge of Egyptian sources, and finally he acknowledges straight-forwardly, that the later Greek philosophy clearly shows traces of Oriental influence.

With regard to the last mentioned fact, he particularly states, that ethic and religious questions were brought more forward, that the ideas on deity became higher and nobler, that new doctrines of a supernatural revelation, of enthusiastic ecstacy in contact with the Divine, of emanation etc. became prevalent in the later philosophical systems that chiefly belonged to Egypt.

It will now become the duty of Egyptologists to bring forward and show which of these ideas may be supposed to be derived from Egypt, a task which is not by any means an easy one, but which however in time will be successfully solved.

Parthey says that the great number of Hellenes, who for the sake of education visited Egypt, more than anything else indicates the essential influence that Egyptian culture, even although only indirectly, has excercised on Hellas, and he gives us a long list of the most prominent Greeks who came to Egypt to study, among whom I need only mention such names as Thales, Pythagoras, Solon, Plato, Herodotus, Diodor and Strabo; he also mentions, likewise from Greek sources, the names of several of their Egyptian teachers. Even if we suppose that this is exaggeration, it is at least evident that Greek authors, who relate this, such as Strabo, Diodor and Plutarch who were themselves acquainted with the Egyptians, must have had high ideas of Egyptian wisdom, when they could admit that their own men of learning had to take long and troublesome journies to profit by it.

Besides this there are a whole number of Greek works the contents of which are principally derived from Egyptian sources to wit Josephus, Plutarch, Porphyrius and Jamblichus, the so-called Maccabæus' 4th book, the hermetic books and others. Plutarchs book on Isis and Osiris shows such knowledge of Egyptian mythology (it has even been used as a fount from which the Egyptologists have drawn) that its author has evidently expended much time and toil in the acquisition of the said knowledge. We have at least here one Greek who has been a scholar in Egypt.

I cited the Maccabæus' 4th book as one of the works containing Egyptian ideas. As a proof in this respect I shall quote the following sentence:

„As a punishment for this (for thy sins) Divine Justice shall prepare thee a strong and eternal fire, and agonies that shall never cease to all eternity.“

We have here manifestly the Egyptian doctrine of hell's fire and torturings. Where else could this idea have come from in a work that is believed to be written by a Hellenised Jew in Alexandria from sixty to eighty years before Christ?

From the foregoing remarks it will be understood that it is impossible for me to agree with the author, when he pretends that neither Jews nor Greeks have borrowed ideas from Egypt. On the contrary I must declare it to be the most important and interesting task for Egyptologists to examine how far, and what ideas have made their way from Egypt, not only into Judaism and Greek literature, but even into Christianity.

However I cannot believe, as I have said before, that the author means it quite as strictly as he expresses himself, for if he did so, he would, as far as I can see, be contradicting himself. He was himself at an earlier period one of those who tried to clear the right way, as he, for instance in 1873, in an acute and decisive manner has shown that medical learning and prescriptions that were in use among the old Egyptians are found again in Hippocrates and later authors, strange to say even in English medical popular works from the latest times.

Lastly, I will make a remark but in a few words, as it concerns a question that has but little to do with religion, I mean chronology. Le Page Renouf deals also but slightly with it, but in such a way that we are tempted to believe that he has not followed with particular interest the investigations of later times on this subject. In this respect he has not advanced further than Dr. Hincks and E. de Rougé; but science has progressed many steps since the time of these learned investigators. I shall only stop a moment to consider Le Page Renouf's remarks about the period of the Hyksos. He says that we know when this ceased, but we do not know when it commenced, or how long it lasted. We have however, by comparing all facts that can here be taken into consideration, believed with good grounds for the presumption that Hyksos made their entry into Egypt at the beginning of the 13th dynasty, that they conquered the Northern part of the country, and ruled there at the same time, as the 13th dynasty reigned in the South. Le Page Renouf calls this a mere hypothesis and is of the opinion that „the presence of important monuments of the Sebekhoteps at Bubastis and Tanis, kings (of the 13th dynasty) whose names occupy an important place in the chamber of Karnak, would alone be sufficient to overthrow this hypothesis,“ at the same time he quotes E. de Rougé as his authority. Now it has long ago been objected against E. de Rougé that Hyksos during their wars with the southern Sebekhoteps may have brought these statues with them to the north as trophies, and the presence of the Sebekhoteps statues in „Bubastis and Tanis“ proves consequently just as little that Sebekhotep has reigned in Bubastis and Tanis as it would occur to any one to pretend, that a Sebekhotep has reigned in Paris because a statue of Sebekhotep is found in the Louvre. The fact mentioned by Le Page Renouf may thus not be „alone sufficient to overthrow this hypothesis.“ On the contrary it is really astonishing that such ·a phantom can appear so long a time after it has been removed. No, entirely other arguments would be required to break the circle of facts corroberating the said hypothesis. I will however not on that account attack our honoured author, the subtle grammarian, who has with his penetrating linguistic works done our science such great services.

Herewith I shall conclude. It may seem that I have maliciously tried to make bare the weak points, but this is not the case. The book is written with so much knowledge of facts and is on the whole so excellent that I can not do otherwise than greet it with delight. I have only considered it my duty to combat several, in my opinion perverse and wrong ideas, that the author's high repute might easily lead to be propagated.